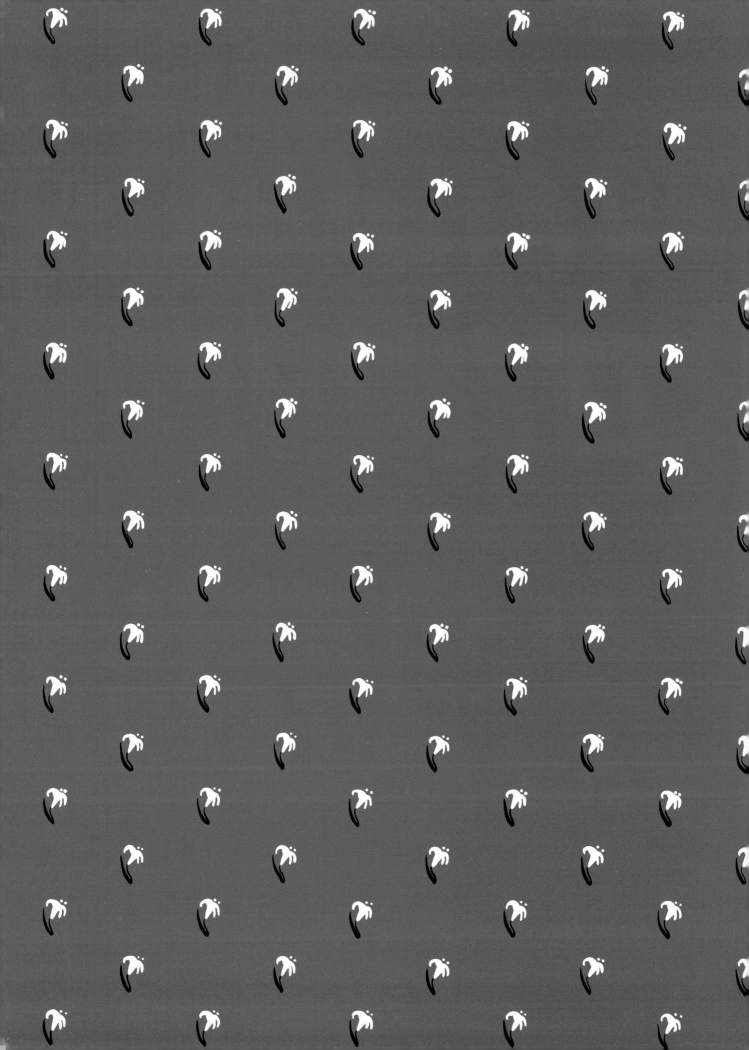

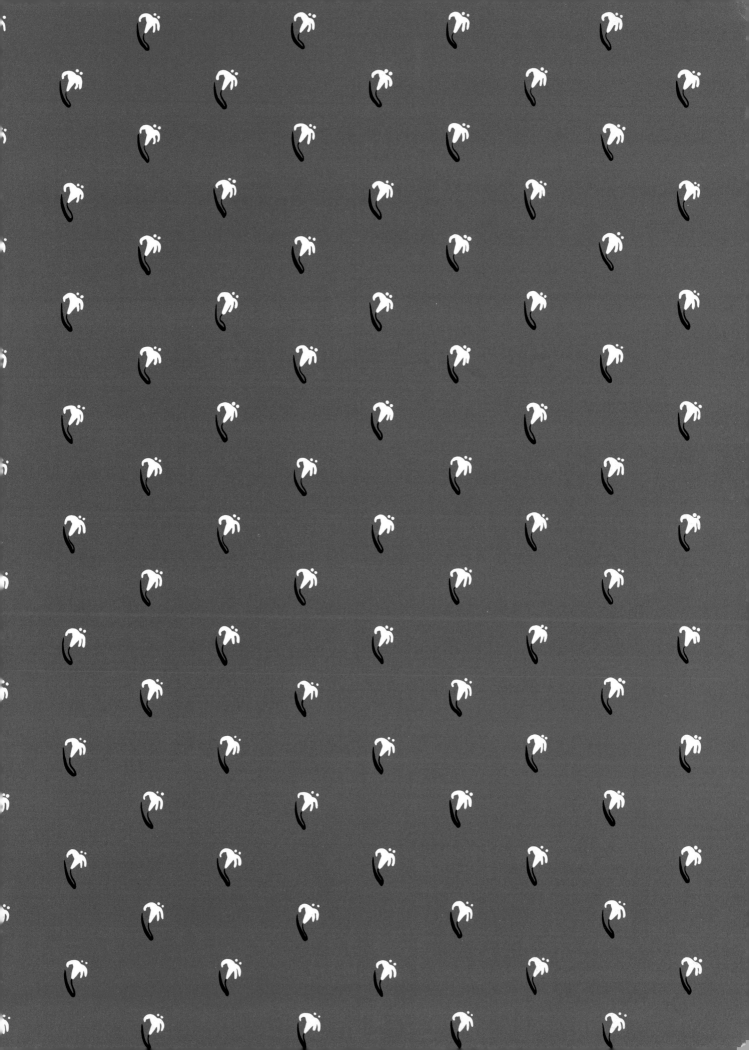

We Celebrate
EASTER

Bobbie Kalman   **Maureen Shaughnessy**

The Holidays & Festivals Series

Crabtree Publishing Company

The Holidays and Festivals Series
Created by Bobbie Kalman

Writing team:
 Bobbie Kalman
 Susan Hughes
 Kathleen Smith

Illustrations:
 Maureen Shaughnessy
 © Crabtree Publishing Company

Editor-in-chief:
 Bobbie Kalman

Editors:
 Susan Hughes
 Lise Gunby
 Grace DeLottinville

Research:
 Kathleen Smith
 Lise Gunby

Cover design:
 Peter Maher, Newton Frank Arthur Inc.
 Karen Harrison

Art direction and design:
 Jane Hamilton
 Hugh Michaelson
 Catherine Johnston
 Ruth Chernia

Mechanicals:
 Nancy Cook

For Pat

Cataloguing in Publication Data
Kalman, Bobbie, 1947-
 We celebrate Easter

(The Holidays and festivals series)
Includes index.
ISBN 0-86505-042-2

1. Easter. I. Title. II. Series.

GT4935.K35 1985   394.2'68283

350 Fifth Avenue   102 Torbrick Avenue
Suite 3308   Toronto, Ontario
New York, N.Y. 10118 Canada M4J 4Z5

Contents

What is Easter?

Easter is a time to be happy.
Easter is a time to celebrate spring
By watching a beautiful sunrise.
Easter is a time for singing and dancing,
And a time for families to share.

Easter is a time for flowers to bloom,
For baby animals to be born,
And for tiny chicks to hatch.
Easter is a time for bunnies
And lots and lots of brightly-colored eggs.

For Christians, Easter is
A time of prayer and rejoicing.
To celebrate Easter means
To remember and celebrate
The life of Jesus Christ.

Easter is a religious holiday.
Easter is a time to enjoy nature.
Easter is a time of newness.
Easter is a time for fun.
Come celebrate Easter with us!

Waiting for spring to come

Which season is your favorite? Do you like winter? Winter can be fun. You can dress in your warmest clothes and play in the snow. You can sit by the window and sip hot chocolate while the wind howls outside. Perhaps the best part of winter, though, is knowing that spring will soon arrive.

A long, long time ago, people did not like the winter season. The days were cold and the nights were long. People had to huddle around a fire to keep warm. They had no fresh food. They were afraid that the food they had grown in the summer would run out during the winter. Worst of all, they were not sure that spring would even come. How would you feel in the wintertime if you thought that spring might not come in March?

Eastre, the goddess of spring

Today, we know that spring always follows winter. In the days of long ago, people believed that a goddess brought the springtime. They called this goddess by different names: Ostara, Osterr, and Eastre. All of these names sound a little alike. What word do they remind you of?

To make sure that the spring goddess returned, people held festivals in her honor. They held these festivals in March. People prayed that Eastre would bring the spring. And guess what? She always did!

People still welcome spring, but they no longer believe in a goddess called Eastre. Today, Easter is the name of a religious festival which occurs in the spring.

Easter is on a different day each year. This is because the date of Easter depends on the cycle of the sun and the moon. However, Easter usually comes between March 22 and April 25.

Join our parade

Here comes Easter. What do you see?
Children in a parade and one of them's me!

Bonnets and baubles, buttons and bows;
My friends are all wearing their very best clothes.

Church bells are ringing, some high and some low.
Flowers are blooming. The grass starts to grow.

The Easter sun shines. I'm glad that it's spring!
I jump into puddles. I hear the birds sing.

Easter has come! What do you see?
Join the parade and have fun with me.

Make your own Easter hat

Would you like to make an Easter hat? Easter hats are fun to make because you can decorate them with things that remind you of spring.

Find a paper pie plate. Decorate the pie plate with tissue-paper flowers or colored paper cut in the shape of flower petals or fruit. Glue ribbons and streamers to the rim of your hat so that they will dangle when you walk. Add anything else to your hat that makes you think of spring and Easter.

Punch two holes in the rim of the plate, one on either side. Cut two pieces of colorful ribbon or string and tie a knot at one end of each piece. Thread the unknotted ends through the holes in your hat. When your Easter hat is finished, you can tie the two ribbons or pieces of string under your chin. Try on your hat. How does it look?

EASTER FUN

How to celebrate Easter and spring

Spring and Easter are times of newness. How can you give your family and friends a gift of newness? Teach a new game to someone younger than you are. Lend a friend your favorite book. Sing a new song to your teacher. Write a poem for your grandparents and read it aloud to them. What other gifts of newness can you give?

Gifts of life

New life grows during the Easter season. Buy the seeds of your favorite flowers. Put the seeds into envelopes. Decorate the envelopes with signs of life such as the sun, flowers, or trees. On the envelope, write the name of the seeds. Draw a picture of the flower that the seeds will become. Give these seed envelopes to your relatives, neighbors, and friends.

Easter cards

Make Easter cards to give to your family and friends. Collect flower petals and put them between sheets of waxed paper. Press the petals in the waxed paper under heavy books for a day or two. When the flower petals are flattened, fold a piece of blank paper in half to make a card. Use a little glue to stick the petals to the front of your card. Write your spring or Easter message inside.

You can also decorate your handmade Easter cards with tissue paper. Cut up small circles of tissue paper. Squeeze them into balls and glue them onto your card. The tissue balls can be blossoms on a tree, flowers in the grass, or little animals in a field. Make fluffy clouds with cotton balls. Draw a picture around the balls.

Paint a mural

Have an Easter or spring celebration with your friends, family, and neighbors. Ask everyone to wear a costume. People can dress up as flowers, religious characters, birds, clouds, or mud puddles.

Arrange to have paints and a long wide sheet of paper at your celebration. Paint a mural about spring or Easter. The mural can also illustrate friendship and world peace. Ask each of your friends to paint a part of the mural. What can you learn about the subject of the mural by looking at the finished painting? What can you learn about your friends?

Show your joy

Sit in a circle and play charades. Everyone must act out a spring or Easter topic. Use topics such as the sun rising and shining, the rock rolling away from Jesus' burial cave, the flowers beginning to grow, or people eating hot cross buns. These topics are explained in this book.

Have some balloons filled with helium. When your party is ending, run outside with your guests and release the balloons into the sky all at once, shouting, ''Happy Easter, happy spring!''

Easter means new life

People around the world celebrate the coming of spring. Signs of new life are everywhere. Easter is a time to be happy. At Easter, Christians remember a very special man who lived long ago.

12

The story of Jesus

Jesus was a kind and peaceful man who loved people. He especially loved children. Some people called Jesus the Prince of Peace. Some called him the Son of God. Jesus taught people about God. Many people trusted and believed in Jesus. They wanted him to teach them ways to please God.

Some people did not like Jesus. They were angry because they did not believe the things he said. One spring day, these people put Jesus on a cross. Jesus died on this dark Friday afternoon. The friends of Jesus were very sad. They prayed that God would take Jesus to heaven.

The body of Jesus was put in a cave. On the Sunday after he died, his friends visited the cave. The cave was empty. Where was Jesus? Later that day, Jesus appeared to some of his friends. He was alive again! Now his followers knew that Jesus was really God's son.

People who believe in Jesus Christ are called Christians. At Eastertime, Christians remember that Jesus came to life again. They celebrate the life of Jesus.

Carnival time

Easter is such a special celebration that people need many days to prepare for it. The days of preparation are called "Lent." The word Lent comes from an old word, "Lenten," which means "springtime."

There are forty days in Lent. Forty is a special number to Christians. A story in the Bible, the book that tells about God, says that Jesus once spent forty days in the wilderness. Jesus stopped eating during this time because he was praying and asking for God's help. Christians think about Jesus during Lent. They try to follow the example he set. Some people stop eating a favorite food for forty days. They think about how to help others.

Good-bye to meat

Before Lent begins, people around the world try to have as much fun as they can because they know that they have forty quiet days ahead. The celebration that comes before Lent has different names. In many countries, this time of fun is called "Carnival," which means "good-bye to meat." Some Christians do not eat meat during Lent. The French call Carnival "Mardi Gras." Other names for Carnival are Karneval, Fasching, Farsang, and Mas.

Colorful parades

Some people begin Carnival celebrations at the beginning of January and celebrate until the first day of Lent. Carnival is a time of parties and dancing. People do silly things during Carnival. They dress in funny costumes and sometimes eat too much! Children throw confetti, flour, and water-filled eggs at one another. They empty the eggshells by poking a small hole in one end of each egg. They fill the empty eggshells with colored water, confetti, or colored flour. Now the fun begins! The children throw the eggs. Their friends are covered with color when the shells break!

14

In some places, Carnival is a huge celebration which includes parades and special events. Two of the most famous carnivals in the world are the Rio Carnival, in Rio de Janeiro, Brazil, and Mardi Gras in New Orleans. Groups of people spend many months making colorful costumes and practicing music and dances for the parade.

In the Carnival parade in Cologne, West Germany, people wear giant papier-mâché heads which are twice the size of their bodies. In Quebec City, Canada, the Winter Carnival celebrations include a big parade and special sporting events such as skating, skiing, and tobogganing.

Party fun

Children have many parties during Carnival. Their homes are decorated with balloons and streamers. Special fried treats such as jelly doughnuts are an important part of the refreshments.

In Germany, children play a game called "chocolate kiss." It is played with chocolate-covered marshmallows. The object of the game is to gobble up marshmallows without allowing others to smear your face with the chocolate. The winner is the person who can eat the most chocolate marshmallows with the cleanest face.

Costumes galore

The best part of Carnival is that children can wear costumes anytime or anyplace for a whole month. How would you have fun if you could wear a costume every day? What costume would you like to wear in a carnival parade?

Shrove Tuesday

Shrove Tuesday is the last Tuesday before Lent. It is a day of feasting. In France, it is called Mardi Gras or Fat Tuesday. In some countries, people stop eating fat during Lent. Perhaps you think fat would not be hard to give up, but fat is used to fry delicious treats, such as doughnuts. On Fat Tuesday, people use up all the fat in their cupboards. In Germany and Austria, people cook *crullers* in the fat. Crullers are thick doughnuts. In Finland, people cook a pancake called *blini*.

Pancake Tuesday

Some people stop eating eggs during Lent. What do they do before Lent to use up all the eggs in their refrigerators? They make pancakes! This is why Shrove Tuesday is also called Pancake Tuesday.

People who live in Olney, a town in England, celebrate this day with a special event. They have had a pancake race on every Shrove Tuesday for over 500 years. Everyone gathers in the center of town. The racers hold frying pans with hot pancakes still cooking in them. At the word "Go!" they dash to the church, flipping their pancakes as they run. They must flip their pancakes at least three times before they reach the church.

Pancake race

Have your own pancake race on Shrove Tuesday. Cut 15 or more pancake-size circles out of cardboard or heavy paper. These will be your pancakes. Cut the heaviest cardboard you can find into the shape of a frying pan. Find two or more friends to join in the race. Agree on a starting point. Before the race begins, place equal numbers of pancakes in piles at an equal distance from the starting point.

When the starting command is given, the players run to their pile of pancakes, pick up a pancake, put it on their frying pan, run back to the starting line, and flip the pancake off the pan. The players repeat this pattern until they have moved their pile of pancakes, one by one, to the starting line. The first player to do this is the winner.

What is the prize? The losers can make some real pancakes for the hungry winners. Follow this easy recipe.

Pancake recipe

500 mL (2 cups) flour
5 mL (1 teaspoon) baking powder
15 mL (1 tablespoon) sugar
2 eggs (beaten)

250 mL (1 cup) milk
30 mL (2 tablespoons) butter
some syrup or jam

1. Mix together flour, baking powder, and sugar.
2. Add beaten eggs to dry ingredients.
3. Stir in milk, and blend until batter is thin enough to be poured.
4. Turn stove element to medium heat. (You should get help from an adult when you are using the stove.) Put frying pan on element and melt a little butter in pan.
5. Use a cup to pour enough batter for one pancake into pan.
6. When top of batter begins to bubble, flip pancake over with a spatula. Try to do this without breaking pancake.
7. When pancake is light brown on both sides, it is cooked. Use rest of batter to make more pancakes.

Serve pancakes hot with butter and jam, maple syrup, or try them the English way, with a squeeze of lemon and a sprinkle of sugar.

The special days of Lent

During the forty days of Lent, there are days with special names. The first day of Lent is called Ash Wednesday. Long ago on this day, Christians dressed in their old clothes. They rubbed ashes on their foreheads. They wanted to show God that they were sorry for the wrong things they had done in the past year. Some Christians today have ashes put on their foreheads at church on Ash Wednesday.

A calendar of Easter week

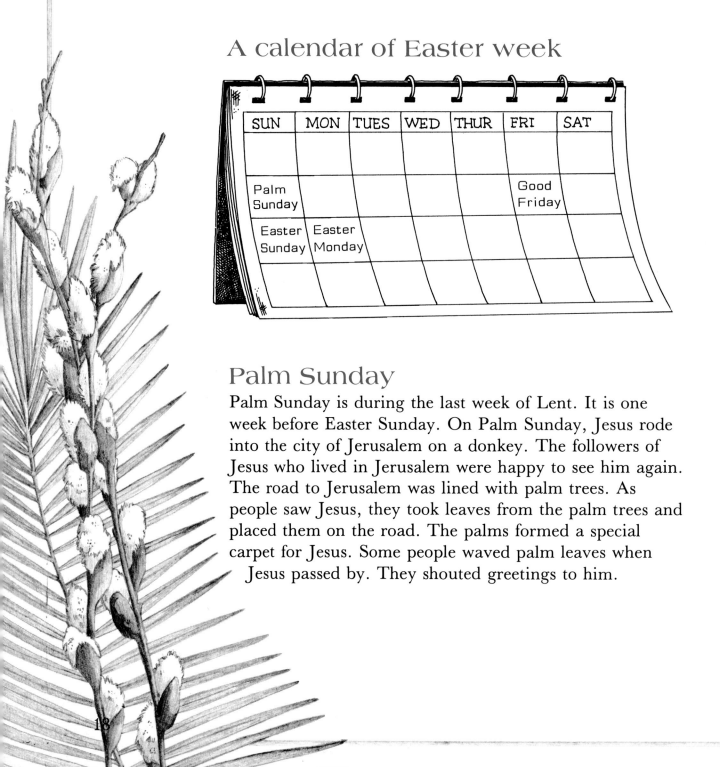

SUN	MON	TUES	WED	THUR	FRI	SAT
Palm Sunday					Good Friday	
Easter Sunday	Easter Monday					

Palm Sunday

Palm Sunday is during the last week of Lent. It is one week before Easter Sunday. On Palm Sunday, Jesus rode into the city of Jerusalem on a donkey. The followers of Jesus who lived in Jerusalem were happy to see him again. The road to Jerusalem was lined with palm trees. As people saw Jesus, they took leaves from the palm trees and placed them on the road. The palms formed a special carpet for Jesus. Some people waved palm leaves when Jesus passed by. They shouted greetings to him.

18

Welcoming Jesus again

Today on Palm Sunday, many Christians go to church. They hold palm leaves to remind them of the time Jesus rode into Jerusalem. They welcome Jesus again into their hearts.

In some countries, it is hard to get palm leaves, so people hold willow or yew branches, or flowers. In Europe, Palm Sunday is called Willow, Yew, or Blossom Sunday.

Good Friday

Good Friday is five days after Palm Sunday. This is a sad day for Christians. It was on this day many years ago that Jesus died. People thought that they would never see Jesus again.

Why is this sad day called "good"? For many years, it was called "God's Friday." God's Friday sounds like Good Friday. This may be the way that Good Friday got its name. In other countries, this day is called Big Friday, Holy Friday, or Silent Friday.

Sad parades

Around the world, Christians have church services on Good Friday. In Spain, Mexico, and many South American countries, there are parades each day of the last week of Lent. The Good Friday parade is the saddest one. The parade of people winds through the dark streets early in the morning. Drums beat and the church bells ring slowly. People in the parade carry large statues of Jesus and his mother, Mary. People crowd the streets to watch the procession go by. They sing sad songs. They sometimes carry candles to brighten the darkness. Everyone is sad on Good Friday, but in two more days it will be Easter Sunday, a time to be happy again.

Easter Sunday

Easter Sunday is a day for rejoicing. It was on Easter Sunday that the friends of Jesus learned that Jesus was alive again. They went to the cave where Jesus had been buried. They found that the huge rock, which blocked the entrance to the cave, had been rolled away. The cave was empty. Jesus was alive again! He promised new life to everyone who believed in him.

Many Christians celebrate the promise of Jesus by going to church on Easter Sunday. They wear their best clothes. Churches are filled with flowers and candlelight. Bells ring out the happiness people feel. Everyone sings joyful hymns. Christians celebrate because Jesus has shown them God's power and love.

Grandmother's Easter flame

"I am sorry you can't go with us tonight, Grandmother," Katina said. "I know that you love the Easter Eve church service." Katina's grandmother smiled at Katina. She patted her granddaughter's hand. "Don't worry, dear," she said. "I will probably be feeling better next Easter. Next year, I can go to church with everyone else. Now hurry along, dear."

Katina kissed her grandmother and ran to join her parents. Together they walked through the dark streets of the little Greek village. They called out greetings to the other people going to church. Katina felt excitement chewing at her stomach. The sadness of Lent was almost over. It would soon be time for happiness and fun.

Katina and her family entered the dark church and found their way to their seats. They could not see much, but they could hear the whispers and shuffling of their neighbors. The church was certainly full on this Easter Saturday night! Katina enjoyed the beautiful church service. She wished that her grandmother was sharing it with her.

The priest cried out, "Christ is risen!" Katina knew then that it must be midnight. Easter Sunday had begun.

Katina held her breath as the priest lit the gigantic Paschal candle which was over three meters high. This was the sign for everyone to pick up the smaller candles brought from home. One by one, people lit their candles, using the flame of the Paschal candle, until all the candles in the church were lit. Katina shivered with delight as her candle flickered and danced. Its flame had been shared by all the people in the church!

Soon the whole church was aglow with candlelight. Katina could see the smiling faces of her friends and neighbors. She could see the blossoms that decorated the church. The singing began and Katina hoped that if she sang loudly enough, her grandmother would hear the Easter hymn from her bedroom.

When the service was over, Katina and her family left the church. Bells were ringing. Fireworks lit up the sky. Katina's parents stopped to talk to their friends, but Katina wanted to hurry home. She was the only one who had not blown out her candle. Her hand was cupped around the flame.

22

Her parents smiled at her. They seemed to know what she was going to do. "Be careful on your way," was all they said.

Katina walked slowly through the streets. She did not want the flame to go out. The Easter flame lit Katina's way through the village. It made her feel safe and warm inside.

Soon, she was standing in the doorway of her grandmother's room. "Wake up, Grandmother," Katina called softly.

"I am awake, dear," Katina's grandmother said. "You look like an Easter angel standing there in the candlelight. Thank you so much for bringing my Easter flame."

Katina placed the candle in the holder beside her grandmother's bed. As she bent over to kiss her grandmother, Katina could see her tears of joy. Easter was truly here!

Easter around the world

Each country has its own special Easter traditions.
Children around the world celebrate in different ways.

Easter in Greece

In Greece, there are outdoor banquets on
Easter Sunday. The feast of barbecued
lamb, eggs, bread, salads, and Easter
cake is spread on long tables for everyone
to enjoy.

Hot cross buns

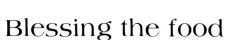

Many people around the world bake
and eat hot cross buns during the
Easter season. This is the only time
of the year when these special buns are
made. Hot cross buns are small, spicy,
sweet buns. They have a white cross of
sugar marked on the top. In the old days,
people ate hot cross buns because they
believed that the buns would keep them
healthy all year.

Blessing the food

In Russia, Christians go to church late on Easter Saturday night. When the
clock strikes midnight, everyone goes outside and walks around the church
three times, singing songs. Then the priest knocks on the church door and
everyone goes back inside. They are happy now because it is Easter
Sunday! The priest blesses the food that the people have brought to church
in baskets. Then everyone goes home to a big feast. They eat lamb,
chicken, pork, bread, and Easter cake. Easter Sunday is a happy day of
eating and visiting.

Easter ham

Hundreds of years ago, people in England began eating ham on Easter
Sunday. This is now a common Easter dish all over the world. Ham comes
from pigs. The pig is a symbol of good luck in many countries. To wish
someone good luck in German is to say ''Schwein haben.'' This means
''have a pig.'' Germans used to believe that it was good luck to own a pig.

Dancing on Easter Sunday

In Spain and Ireland, people dance in the streets on Easter Sunday. The dancers compete for the prize of a cake. In some parts of England, these springtime dancers are called "Morris dancers." They wear white shirts and red sashes. They have straw hats with streamers that dip and curl when they dance. Red and green ribbons are tied above the knees of their black trousers. Rows of little bells jingle as the dancers perform. The Morris dance is hundreds of years old.

Easter witches?

In Sweden, children celebrate Easter in a special way. They draw pictures of witches on pieces of paper and add Easter greetings to the pictures. Then, dressed as witches, the children deliver their Easter cards to the homes of their friends. Firecrackers are set off in the streets as the children run from one mailbox to the next. The witches stand for bad luck and the firecrackers are lit to frighten the bad luck away.

Easter words

Try to use all these words to write your own Easter story.

candles

Morris dancers

Easter
sunrise

church

Easter
bonnet

rabbit

chicks

basket

bells

Eastre
(spring goddess)

Carnival
costume

Paschal candle

rock

cave

cross

pussy willows

Easter lilies

palm

ham

pancakes

hot cross buns

pysanky

eggs

chariot

27

The miracle of eggs

"Hey! There's an earthquake in that egg!" cried Jody. Sure enough, the white egg on the table was shaking. Jody and her friends stared in amazement as the egg began to break apart before their eyes.

"There's a knife inside that egg!" shouted Lee. "No," said Susan. "It's not a knife. It's a little hammer!" "You're both wrong," said Roger. "There's a grasshopper with a spear in there!"

As the egg fell apart bit by bit, the children saw a baby chick come pecking its way out of the eggshell. The yellow bird took its first shaky steps outside the shell and greeted the children: "Cheep, cheep!"

Slowly the other eggs began to shake and break. Before the children knew it, twelve tiny chicks had hatched before their eyes.

28

How do eggs hatch?

How do baby birds break out of their eggs? Some birds have a *hatching muscle* and an *egg tooth*. When the bird is ready to hatch, the hatching muscle tightens. It pulls up the bird's head so that the bird's beak hits the shell. On the top of the beak is the egg tooth. This is a little pointed bump. When the bird's beak hits the shell, the egg tooth cracks the shell. The bird pecks at the shell until it opens. After the baby bird climbs out of the shell, the hatching muscle shrinks and the egg tooth drops off.

Easter eggs

Why are eggs so popular at Easter? Eggs remind people of life. An egg seems lifeless, but then out pops a baby bird! Eggs remind people of spring. The earth in winter appears lifeless, but then spring comes!

29

Egg-citing trivia about eggs

Eggs have always been important to people, and not just at Easter. Many kinds of birds, fish, and reptiles hatch from eggs.

There are many stories, poems, and riddles about eggs. Have you heard any of these?

An eggs-tremely bad fall

Do you know this rhyme about a famous egg?

Humpty Dumpty sat on a wall,
Humpty Dumpty had a great fall.
All the Queen's horses and all the Queen's men
Could not put Humpty together again.

Can anyone put an egg together after it breaks?

Try this eggs-periment

Can you squeeze an egg in your fist without breaking it? Try it, but do not dig your fingernails into the shell or the egg *will* break.

An Eggs-pensive mistake

Do you know the old story about the goose that laid the golden eggs?

Once upon a time, there was a man who went to market and bought a goose. The goose was a very special goose. It laid golden eggs! The man was thrilled with his goose. He collected one golden egg each morning. He took the fresh golden egg to the market every day. He traded it for other things he needed.

One day the man thought to himself, "Why should I have to wait for my egg each day? Wouldn't it be nice if I could have all the golden eggs at once?" So, the man killed his goose. He looked inside it for the golden eggs. There were no eggs.

"Oh me, oh my. I did not find any golden eggs," the man cried, "I have killed the goose that laid the golden eggs. Why, oh why, was I so greedy? I used to have one golden egg every day. Now I have none."

30

Eggs-plaining how the world was made

There are many old stories about eggs. Long, long ago, many people believed that the world was created from a giant egg and that the sun was the yolk of this egg. The ancient people of Hawaii thought that this giant egg burst and its pieces formed the Hawaiian Islands.

Eggs-actly!

Do you know the answer to this old riddle?
> What has neither head nor foot,
> Neither arms nor tail?
> What is neither living nor dead?

Did you guess? Why, of course you did. An egg!

Eggs-amine this carefully

How can you tell a hard-boiled egg from a raw egg?

Spin the egg carefully on a flat surface. Raw eggs hardly spin at all. The yolk and egg white inside the egg are not hard. They are soft, and slosh about when the egg spins. This slows down the movement of the egg. A hard-boiled egg spins quickly. The inside of the egg is hard. It spins at the same speed as the shell.

Do you know this eggs-pression?

''Do not put all your eggs in one basket.'' This means that it is a bad idea to pin all your hopes (eggs) on one event or project (basket). If you are disappointed about this one event, you are left with no hopes (your eggs are shattered).

High eggs-pectations

''Don't count your chickens before they are hatched.'' What does this expression mean? This means that it is a bad idea to count on things before they actually happen. You should not try to count the number of chicks you will have if they have not hatched from the eggs yet. Not all eggs hatch. Not all plans succeed.

The Easter bells

In France and Italy, church bells ring joyfully during the year. But the bells stop ringing on the Thursday before Good Friday. They are silent for a few days while people remember the death of Jesus. On Easter Sunday morning, the bells ring out, telling people that Jesus is alive again. When people hear the bells, they kiss and hug one another.

Many children wake up on Easter Sunday and find eggs scattered about their rooms. They look in the nests they have placed in their yards or gardens and find Easter eggs in them. Where did the eggs come from?

Eggs in the sky?

Children are told that the silent bells fly to Rome on the Thursday before Good Friday. They go to Rome to see the Pope, the head of the Roman Catholic church. When the ringing bells return on Easter Sunday, they bring Easter eggs. Some parents take their children to hilltops to watch for the flying bells.

Belgian children watch for an old man who flies with the bells to Rome to collect eggs from the Pope. In some parts of France and Italy, children look for four white horses pulling a chariot full of eggs. Do you think the children ever see the flying bells, the old man, or the chariot? Have you ever seen the Easter Bunny?

Decorating Easter eggs

People have been decorating eggs at Eastertime for hundreds of years. You can decorate eggs in the traditional way too. First, blow the inside of the egg out of the shell. Make a small hole in one end of the egg using a needle. Make a larger hole in the other end. Hold the egg over a bowl and blow steadily into the small hole. The contents of the egg will come out of the larger hole. Rinse the inside of the eggshell with water and let it dry.

While the eggshell is drying, you can make the dye. Dyes can be made from simple things. What color would you like your egg to be? Yellow dye can be made from onion skins, goldenrod stems and leaves, or leaves from a pear tree. Use red onion skins or the juice from fresh beets for a red dye. Use spinach, rhubarb leaves, or moss for a green dye.

Wash the dye material you have chosen. If you are using leaves, chop them into fine pieces. Put the material in a pot and cover it with water. Boil the water gently for 5 minutes or longer. Place an old piece of bedsheet or a piece of cheesecloth in a strainer. Strain the dye through the cloth and the strainer into a bowl. Pour some of the dye into a cup. Add a teaspoonful of vinegar to each cup of dye (unless the dye is made from onion skins, which do not need vinegar). Use a spoon to dip the egg into the dye. The richness of the color will depend upon the length of time you leave the egg in the dye.

Ukrainian designs

Ukrainians decorate eggs in a special way called *pysanky*. They make beautiful designs with beeswax on eggs. The beeswax is melted and a special *stylus* or pen is dipped in the wax. A wax design is painted onto the egg with the stylus. Then the egg is dipped in dye. The dyed egg is carefully held over a candle flame and the wax melted off. Now, there is a beautiful white pattern on the dyed egg.

Ukrainian egg designs are very delicate and complicated. The patterns for the designs are passed down from parents to children over the years.

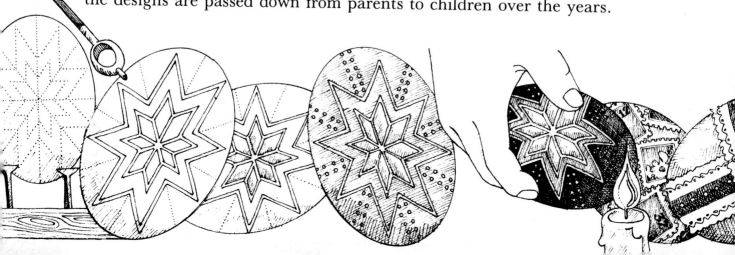

Try pysanky

Try a simple form of pysanky. Design a pattern on a piece of white paper. Try a simple design first. Now, use a wax crayon to draw your design onto the egg.

Fill a cup with water and add a teaspoonful of vinegar to it. What color do you want your egg to be? Add a few drops of the food coloring of your choice to the water and vinegar until you get the shade of color you like.

Put the egg that you have crayoned into the dye and let it soak. When the egg is the color you want it to be, take it out of the dye and let it dry. Your colored egg now has a beautiful crayon design on it.

Use rug yarn

In Poland, it is the custom to decorate eggs with rug yarn. You can try this method. Draw a pattern for your egg on a piece of paper. You will need to cut pieces of yarn to match your pattern. Working with one half of the egg at a time makes the egg easier to handle. Cover half of the egg in glue or rubber cement. Now, copy your design onto the egg by gluing the colored pieces of yarn in place. When one half of the egg is done, repeat the method on the other half of your egg.

Do it your way

Invent egg-decorating methods of your own. You can use anything to decorate eggs. Dribble glue in a pattern on an egg. Now, drop colorful glitter on the egg. It will stick to the glue and make your egg sparkle! Stick on old postage stamps, stars, or stickers. Glue sea shells, pasta, or paper shapes on your eggs. Paint your eggs or draw on them with crayon. You can even use felt markers.

You do not have to decorate real eggs at Easter. Styrofoam eggs from a craft store can make pretty Easter eggs. Glue decorations or paint pictures on them. Pin sequins, beads, or ribbons to them. The best thing about styrofoam eggs is that they won't break!

The Easter sunrise

The custom of watching the sunrise on Easter Sunday morning is a very old one. Thousands of years ago, people called the spring goddess Eastre. Eastre means ''to rise.'' Perhaps people thought of the sun rising when they celebrated spring. People still think of the sunrise at Easter. The bright sun brings a beautiful new day of hope.

Sleepyhead Edward

Edward loved to sleep. He loved to stay in bed all morning. Sometimes on the weekend, Edward's parents allowed him to sleep in. But not this morning! Edward was awakened by his mother's soft voice. "It's time to get up, Edward. It's Easter Sunday. We're going to the park to watch the sun rise."

Edward opened one eyelid. His room was still very dark. He yawned. "But Mom, the sun isn't up yet. The birds aren't even awake! I don't want to get up, Mom. I want to sleep."

"Edward, of course the sun isn't up. We're going to watch it rise. This is a special day. No sleeping in today!"

Edward closed his eyes. He started to drift back to sleep. "Come on, sleepyhead!" said his mother. "Welcome the sun with us."

Half an hour later, Edward was standing on a hill in the park with his parents, neighbors, and friends. They all watched the sky. Edward yawned. His eyes kept trying to close.

Suddenly, someone shouted, "Look, look. It's the Easter sun!" Edward opened his tired eyes. The sun was peeking out from behind the buildings of the town. Everyone on the little hilltop started to sing an Easter song.

Edward felt wide awake now. He was glad to have seen the sun come up. He was glad that this was just the beginning of Easter Sunday. Waking up before the sun wasn't so bad after all. It made good days last longer! Soon Edward would be going home to search his garden for Easter eggs. His whole family would be coming for Easter dinner. Today would be a special day indeed!

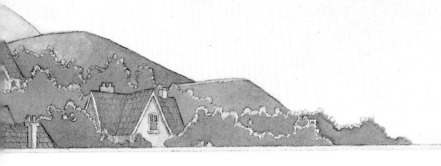

The Easter Bunny

In many countries, children believe that the Easter Bunny leaves them colored eggs, chocolate bunnies, and candy on Easter Sunday. This belief may have started thousands of years ago. People celebrated springtime with festivals for Eastre, the goddess of spring. Eastre's favorite animal was the hare. A hare is an animal similar to a rabbit. Easter and rabbits have gone together for a long time!

Easter morning madness

Ben Bunny scratched his long, gray ears. "Now where did I put it?" he wondered to himself. It was very early on Easter morning and Ben had lost something. He couldn't even remember what he had lost. His pink nose wiggled.

"Let's see now," Ben said. "It's Easter morning. I do know that. Red Robin woke me up this morning. He told me that I had work to do." Ben glanced around his underground home. There were top hats everywhere. Ben Bunny collected top hats. Some were gray. Some were black. And some had ribbons, too.

Ben peered under some of the hats. "I wish I could remember what I have lost," he muttered. "Maybe Red Robin can help me." Ben went up his front tunnel, plopping his favorite gray top hat between his ears.

On his way to Red Robin's tree, Ben saw his friend Edward in the distance. Edward was waiting with his family and friends for the first rays of the Easter sun. "I have a feeling I should hurry," Ben said to himself. "I have a feeling my work is supposed to be done very soon." He hopped off in a hurry toward Red Robin's tree.

Red Robin was sitting in his nest whistling a tune. "Help me, Red Robin," said Ben. "What am I supposed to be doing this morning? Do you know?" Ben straightened his top hat. It had fallen a little to one side.

Red Robin scolded, "You're the Easter Bunny. You're supposed to deliver Easter eggs. You'd better get moving. The sun is coming up!"

"You're right! Now I remember," Ben cried out excitedly. "And what I have lost are my Easter eggs. Have you seen them anywhere, Red Robin?"

"Yes, dear Ben," Red Robin sighed. "They are in the meadow near the house of Jenny Mouse. That is where you always keep your Easter eggs."

"Thank you, thank you, and happy Easter, Red Robin," Ben called as he raced toward the meadow. "Now I must hurry if I am to deliver those Easter eggs on time."

A meadow of Easter eggs

The sun was just beginning to show through the trees when Ben Bunny reached the meadow. What a sight greeted his pink-rimmed eyes! There were eggs everywhere! They were all colors and all sizes. Some were painted with tiny pictures. Some were made of chocolate. Some were even wrapped in shiny pink and blue paper.

Jenny Mouse popped out of her house. ''Well, Ben Bunny, you've got your work cut out for you this morning. Did you bring your basket?'' Ben Bunny's ears drooped sadly. ''I left my Easter basket at home. How am I going to collect all these eggs?''

''Why don't you use your hat?'' asked Jenny. Ben hopped up and down. ''That's a great idea, Jenny. If I hurry, I can do my job before Edward gets home from watching the sunrise.''

Ben stuffed his top hat full of eggs and raced toward
Edward's house. Suddenly, he stopped in his tracks. ''I've
forgotten where I'm supposed to put these eggs.''

Ben began scattering the Easter eggs throughout the
garden. He hid some in the bushes. He placed some in the
flowers. He put some under the lawn furniture. When the
job was done, Ben wiped his forehead. ''Whew! It's tough
work being the Easter Bunny,'' he said. He scratched a
long, gray ear. ''Now, where did I leave my hat?'' he said
to himself.

Easter recipes

Easter is a time for feasting. There are many recipes for fun Easter foods. Make an Easter Rabbit Salad, Edible Easter Baskets, or Ben's Best Chocolate Eggs. Enjoy them with a friend. These recipes will keep you both hopping!

Easter Rabbit Salad

1 pear
1 leaf of lettuce or cabbage
1 carrot
2 small candies (or red currants or raspberries)
1 marshmallow (small or large)
melted chocolate
1 caramel (or a slice of licorice)

1. Peel a pear. Cut it in half lengthwise and slice out the core. One pear half makes the rabbit's body.
2. Place the pear half on a lettuce or cabbage leaf. The narrow end of the pear is the rabbit's head.
3. Cut two long diagonal slices of carrot. These are the rabbit's ears. Make small cuts on either side of the rabbit's head. Stand the carrot slices up in these, as shown in the picture.

4. Use two small red candies, red currants, or raspberries for the rabbit's eyes.
5. Use a small marshmallow or cut a piece of large marshmallow for the rabbit's tail. Place the tail at the fat end of the pear.
6. Dribble melted chocolate onto the rabbit in the shape of a jacket.
7. Use a caramel or a slice of licorice to make a top hat for the rabbit. Does he look like Ben Bunny?

Edible Easter Baskets

750 mL (3 cups) miniature marshmallows
60 mL (1/4 cup) butter
1.5 L (5-6 cups) rice cereal
jelly beans
chocolate eggs
candies

1. Melt marshmallows and butter in a double boiler.
2. Pour into a bowl and add rice cereal. Stir until cereal is evenly coated.

3. Allow mixture to cool.
4. Lightly butter several cereal bowls.
5. Spoon mixture into bowls until bowls are three-quarters full.
6. Grease the bottom of a drinking glass. To make basket shapes, press and twist greased glass bottom into mixture in each bowl.
7. Refrigerate bowls.
8. When baskets have hardened, remove them from bowls.
9. Fill with jelly beans, chocolate eggs, or candies.
Make the Easter season sweet!

Ben's Best Chocolate Eggs

125 mL (1/2 cup) white margarine
7.5 mL (1 1/2 teaspoons) vanilla
250 mL (1 cup) sweetened
  condensed milk
1 L (4 cups) icing sugar
yellow food coloring

1. Cream together margarine and vanilla.
2. Add condensed milk and blend together well (if possible, use a blender).
3. Gradually add icing sugar.
4. Knead mixture until it is smooth and not sticky. Add more icing sugar if mixture is too moist.
5. Place on a piece of waxed paper.
6. Separate 1/3 of mixture. Color this portion with yellow food coloring, adding a few drops at a time until mixture is a bright yellow.
7. Roll mixture into 2 1/2 cm (1 inch) yellow balls. These are the yolks.
8. Mold parts of white mixture around yellow yolks.
9. Let eggs harden for a day, turning them over once. After eggs harden, make chocolate coating.

Chocolate coating

250 mL - 500 mL (1-2 cups) semi-
  sweet chocolate

1. Melt chocolate.
2. Hold eggs with prongs or two forks and dip into chocolate.
3. Put chocolate-covered eggs aside to set. When set, decorate with ornamental frosting. Wrap eggs in aluminum foil and hide them around your home or place them in Easter baskets. You can help Ben bring Easter eggs to your family and friends on Easter morning.

Easter hunt

Help Edward find his Easter eggs. Ben the
Easter Bunny has put them in some very
unusual places! Can you spot all 35 eggs
hidden in the picture below? You may have
to turn the book upside down or stand on
your head to find some of them!

Easter crafts

Celebrate Easter with these special activities and crafts.

Easter puppets

Make a bunny puppet. Find a small brown paper bag. This will be the body of your puppet. Cut long ears, a nose, and whiskers out of colored construction paper and glue them to the bag. Glue a white cotton ball on the back of the bag. This is the bunny's tail.

Make a chicken puppet for Easter. First, make the beak. Cut two triangles out of cardboard or construction paper. Make a small fold along an edge of each triangle. Glue the triangles by their folds onto the bag so that they stick out from the bag. Cut eye shapes from blue, brown or black construction paper and glue onto the bag. Cut the chicken's comb out of red construction paper. Glue it to the bag by folding and then gluing a section of it in the same way you folded the beak. Your chicken puppet needs wings. Cut wings out of colored construction paper or color white paper to look like feathers. Attach them to your puppet. Wear your puppet on your hand. Now your chicken is ready to fly!

Make a mask

Make an Easter face mask using a paper plate. Make holes for your eyes and your nose. Cut string or yarn for hair, and glue it to the top of the mask. Add freckles, rosy cheeks, and a smiling mouth using glued paper or crayons. Punch a hole in the rim on each side of your mask. Tie a string to each hole. Use these strings to tie the mask around your head. Can anyone recognize you behind your Easter mask?

Your very own egg tree

Blow out the insides of several eggs (as described on page 34). Rinse each empty egg with water and let it dry. Decorate the eggs (you can use the decorating suggestions in this book or invent your own methods).

Look for a fallen tree branch in your neighborhood. Try to find a long, strong branch that has some smaller branches on it. Strip off any dead leaves. Fill a large pail, tin can, or other container with sand and pebbles. The container must be big enough to support your branch. If you have plaster of Paris, add it to the container. Place the branch in the container and make certain it will stand securely.

Decorate the tree. Tie a short thread or string around the middle of a toothpick. Push the toothpick through the larger hole in one of your eggs. Hold the loose end of the thread or string. Give it a gentle pull. The toothpick should remain inside the egg. The egg will dangle from the thread or string. Do this with all the eggs. Tie the decorated eggs to the branch. What a pretty egg tree you have made!

Eggshell mosaics

A mosaic is a design or pattern made with small objects or bits of objects. Peel the shell of hard-boiled eggs. Put all the eggshells into a bowl and crush them. Put some of the crushed eggshells in a paper cup or a small glass. Add a few drops of food coloring. Stir the eggshells until they are colored by the dye. Empty the shells onto a paper towel and let them dry.

Wash out the cup or glass. Put more pieces of the white shell in the cup or glass and dye them with a different color food coloring. Do the same thing again with another color. Use at least three or four colors.

Cut out a piece of construction paper. Drip white all-purpose glue onto the paper in a pattern. Sprinkle the colored eggshells onto the glue. When the glue dries, blow off the loose eggshells. You will have a pretty eggshell mosaic.

Easter Monday

Spring is a time for rain showers, but Easter Monday can be a wet day for other reasons! Long ago, people believed that water was special during Easter. Girls washed their faces in streams or in the morning dew. They believed that this would make them beautiful!

Spray, sprinkle, and splash!

In parts of Europe, Easter Monday was a day for pushing friends into the water. Because of this, in Hungary, this day was called Ducking Monday. Today in Hungary, boys sprinkle girls with perfume or perfumed water. They wish one another good luck. The girls must reward the boys who spray them. They give them coins or Easter eggs.

Lifting and heaving

In England, a favorite custom on Easter Monday and Tuesday was called "lifting" or "heaving." Young men went from home to home in the village. They carried a chair decorated with flowers. When a girl or a woman sat in the chair, they lifted her into the air three times. Being lifted was supposed to bring her good luck. She thanked the young men with money and a kiss! On the Tuesday following Easter Monday, it was the women's turn to lift the men in a chair!

How did this custom start? Some people think that it started as a wish that the crops would grow tall. Others believe that the custom began as a reminder that Jesus was lifted from the grave and taken to heaven.

Easter games

Knock Eggs

In Europe and Australia, children play a funny Easter game. They "knock eggs." You can play this game with your friends on Easter Monday. Each player must have one egg. The best eggs for this game are hard-boiled and dyed. The players line up in two rows facing each other.

Each player holds an egg firmly in one fist so that everyone can see one end of the egg. The players in one row knock or hit the eggs of the players in the opposite row. If a player hits someone's egg too hard, his or her own egg will break! If the opponent's egg does not break after seven knocks, the opponent takes a turn knocking the first player's egg. The knocking continues until one of the eggs breaks. The winners in each row must now play against each other. These play-offs go on until there is only one unbroken egg left. This is the winning egg.

Egg Toss

Egg Toss should be played outdoors. The eggs can be raw or hard-boiled. Players stand in a large circle. Each player has an egg. One by one, each player tosses the egg into the air and tries to catch it without breaking it. Those whose eggs break are out of the game. Those who stay in the game after the first round must now throw their eggs higher. As the circle gets smaller, the eggs fly higher into the air. This is a messy game when played with raw eggs, so keep wet towels and cloths handy!

Egg Gathering

Egg Gathering is a popular outdoor game in Germany. A long stretch of grass or track is needed for this race. Colored, hard-boiled eggs are placed in a line down the stretch of the grass or track. There must be a line of eggs for each racer. The lines should have equal numbers of eggs.

Each racer holds a basket and stands at the start of a line of eggs. When the word "Go!" is shouted, each racer runs down a line of eggs, picking up the eggs in the line and putting them into the basket. The winner is the first one to cross the finish line with all the eggs from his or her line collected in the basket.

Egg Relay

Try this relay with two or three teams of four or more players. Each team lines up at the starting point. The first person in each line is given a basket with three hard-boiled eggs. When the command to start is given, the first person in each line picks up an egg and holds it under his or her chin. After an egg is taken from the basket and put under the first player's chin, the players must not touch the egg with their hands until it has been passed to the last player. They must use only their chin and neck to hold and pass the egg. It is not easy! As soon as the first egg is passed, the first person in line gets ready to pass the second egg. When three eggs have been passed down the line, the team sits down. The first team to sit down wins the relay.

51

Egg Rolling

Easter Monday is a day of happiness. People want to sing and jump and run and laugh. Easter Monday is a time for games, and most of these games are played with eggs. In Europe and the United States, a popular game is Egg Rolling. Eggs of every color are rolled down hills. Whose egg will still be in one piece when it reaches the bottom of the hill? In some countries, a small slide or track is made of wood. Players take turns rolling eggs down this slide.

No one knows for sure how the custom of egg rolling began. Some people believe that rolling eggs reminds people of the happy day when the stone in front of Jesus' burial cave was rolled away.

Easter Monday at the White House

Easter Monday is an important day at the White House, the home of the President of the United States. The President and the President's family invite children to roll eggs down the green hill outside their home. Children arrive wearing their best clothes. They carry decorated baskets full of colored eggs. A band plays music. The members of the President's family talk to the children and shake hands with them. Finally, the children roll their eggs down the slopes on the lawn. What a great way to celebrate Easter Monday!

52

53

Easter symbols

There are many things that remind us of Easter. These special things are called symbols. When you think of Easter, do visions of eggs and bunnies pop into your head? Easter has many symbols. Some of these symbols remind people of Jesus Christ. Other symbols came from very old spring festivals and have become a part of Easter celebrations.

The Cross

Many people around the world believe that Jesus died and came back to life again. These people belong to many different churches. However, they are all Christians. The symbol for Christian religions is the cross. Jesus died on the cross and came back to life on the very first Easter Sunday.

The Easter lily

The Easter lily is a beautiful flower which grows from a lifeless-looking bulb. The growth of the tall, white Easter lily reminds Christians of the way Jesus came back to life.

The Easter lily was first seen on the small islands south of Japan. From there, it was taken to Bermuda where it grew well in the tropical climate. It was then brought to North America to be grown in greenhouses for the Easter season. The Easter lily is shaped like a trumpet. It ''blows'' a welcome to spring.

Easter flowers

Other flowers which make us think of Easter are the daffodil, narcissus, and tulip. All of these start as bulbs and bloom into beautiful flowers in the spring.

Pussy willows

In England and Russia, pussy willow branches are picked especially for Easter. People tap each other with them for good luck.

Lambs

Christians often speak of Jesus as the Good Shepherd who looks after people, who are his lambs. Jesus is also known as the Lamb of God. In the old days, it was considered lucky to see a lamb on Easter Sunday.

Rabbits

Rabbits are known for the many baby bunnies they have. They remind us of new life. Rabbits also remind us of spring, because the hare, which looks like a rabbit, was the favorite animal of the spring goddess Eastre.

The egg

Eggs are a symbol of both Easter and spring. Eggs look lifeless. However, many living creatures hatch from eggs. Eggs are a symbol of new life.

Chicks

Chicks are born from eggs. They remind us of spring and of Easter.

What are your favorite Easter symbols?

Perhaps you have your very own symbols which remind you of Easter and spring. Whatever these symbols are, they are important because they mean something special to *you*.

The spirit of Easter

The Easter feeling does not end.
It signals a new beginning,
Of nature, spring, and brand new life,
And friendship, peace, and giving.
The spirit of Easter is all about
Hope, love, and joyful living.

Index

3456789 BP Printed in Canada 4321098

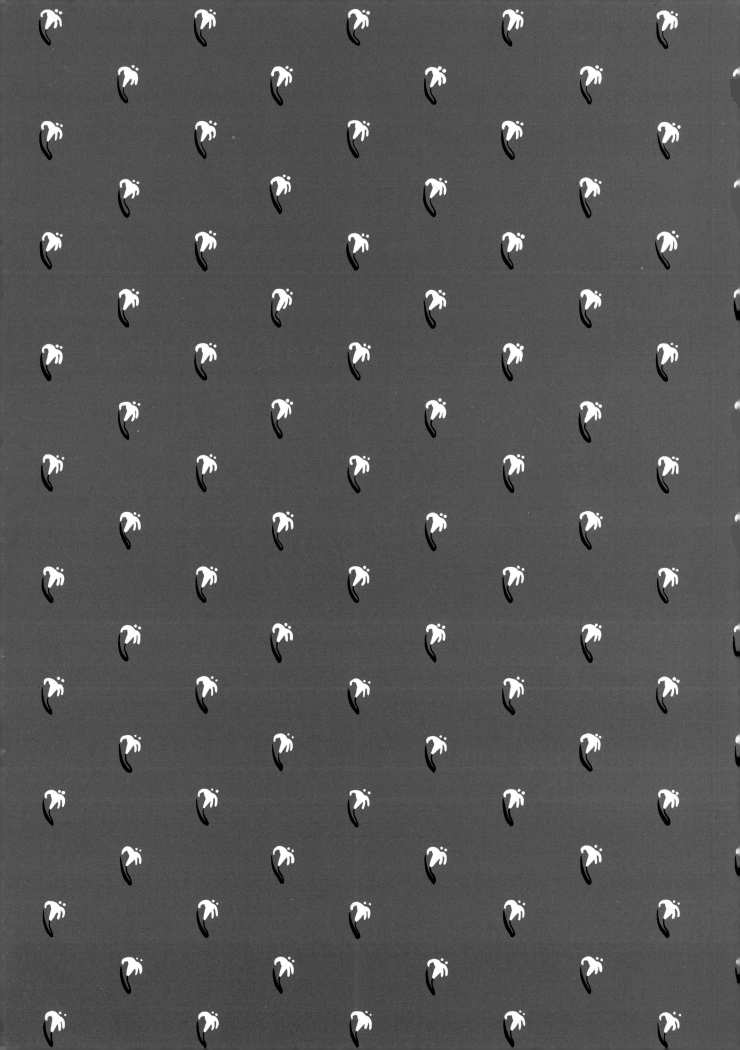

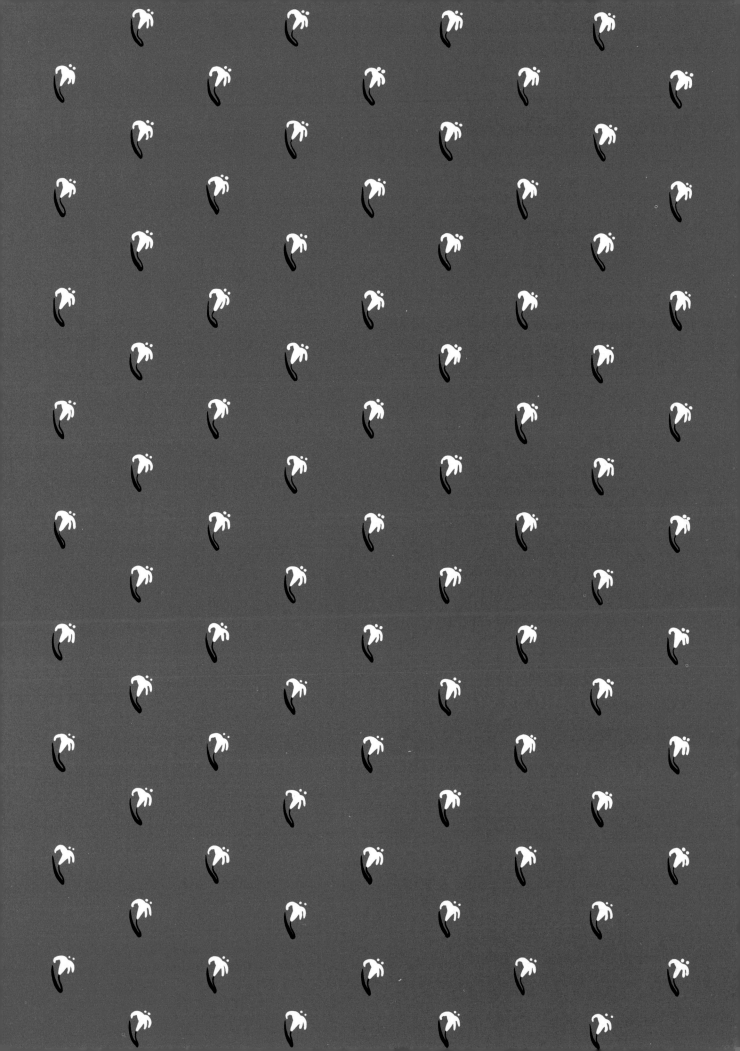